Other books in the Sufism Lecture Series:

Sufism

Molana Salaheddin Ali Nader Shah Angha
"Pir Oveyssi"

University of Hamburg
November 3, 1994

M.T.O. Shahmaghsoudi® Publications

M.T.O. Shahmaghsoudi® Publications

Angha, Salaheddin Ali Nader Shah

Sufism

Library of Congress Catalog Card Number: 95-077987
ISBN: 0-910735-98-0

Printed in the U.S.A.

Published and distributed by M.T.O. Shahmaghsoudi
P.O. Box 5827
Washington, D.C. 20016
U.S.A.

website: http://mto.shahmaghsoudi.org

✯ ✯ ✯ ✯

Contents

✯ ✯ ✯ ✯

Wherever the masculine gender is used, it is solely for the purpose of linguistic convenience. Since the intent of religion is for the spiritual elevation of each individual, we believe that religion addresses the soul, and the soul is not subject to gender classification.

Introduction

A few years ago Hazrat Pir began one of his lectures by asking the audience these questions, "If there were only one in the world, and that one were you, what would be your name? Who would you be? Would you hate? Would you love?" Only an instant lapsed before he calmly asked, "If there were one, and that one had all the knowledge of the universe, and could respond to all your needs and all your wants, what would you do?" Then he said, Sufism is about this "ONE".

Hazrat Pir's method of teaching is definitely thought provoking, and his students say demanding and challenging. Some say he evokes the same system of learning as Socrates did with his students. Those who have interviewed him usually confess that they are totally disarmed by his questions, becoming engaged in an intense learning experience. True to his mission, Hazrat Pir never ceases to teach. His main goal is to show people how they may attain the true state of human dignity, peace and tranquility. His definition of the human being rises above social, cultural and psychological definitions.

Sophisticated communication systems have linked people worldwide, breaking down the "absolutes" that societies, communities and countries had defined and kept sacred for themselves. It is the age of relativity. While exposure to diversity has expanded people's vision of the world, it has also brought elements of insecurity and instability into the day-to-day life of many people. When standards collapse and values shift, where can we find the ultimate definition of our "self"?

Hazrat Pir says, "Each person is a complex and unique masterpiece." Most people, if not all, would like this statement to be true. But what prevents us from experiencing it? What must happen for us to even understand the magnitude of this statement? If we don't allow our imagination to quickly define it, package it and file it away, we could start on a powerful journey of self-realization, which would change the entire fabric of societies, human interactions and legal and social systems. This means moving through the multidimensional patterns of social conditionings that have structured our lives, formed our identities, personalities, self-worth, our perceptions of others and our value systems.

How can we put these aside? And if we should put them aside what would be the yardstick with which we could measure our achievements, our knowledge and our understanding of anything?

Hazrat Pir says, "You are the measure for everything." He is often heard saying, "You have everything that you need. All you need to do is to lift the boundaries you have created, then 'reality' will unveil." But if one wants to be this "unique masterpiece", how, realistically, does one "lift the boundaries?"

"Know thyself," wrote the philosopher Plato about integrity; because "an unexamined life is not worth living." From the time of the Greeks, Western philosophy has advocated self-knowledge — internal learning. Internal learning is at the heart of Islam. As the Holy Prophet Muhammad has said, "Whoever knows the true self knows God."

To begin at the beginning — know thyself. The "i", the individual, is a cherished concept, the acknowledged foundation upon which democracy is built. By transforming the "i", one can go a long way towards transforming the greater world in which the "i" lives. The belief in the perfectibility of the Self has strengthened the fiber of Western society and the collapse of this belief in the twentieth century has brought about alienation and uncertainty in modern societies. Untouched by today's social, economic and political shifts, Hazrat Pir represents a strong and clear voice, reminding us of the urgency to know the true and stable "I". In so doing, he reaffirms the human being's capacity to master the self.

One of the significant contributions of Hazrat Pir to the reservoir of world knowledge is the idea that, because the world has projected its divisions and boundaries onto the vulnerable "i", one must create a process for achieving mastery of mind. This is done by first removing these divisions and boundaries onto the "i" through an inner experience of religion that begins with spiritual integration and ends with a complete metamorphosis. It is no coincidence that two of the healthiest and strongest mystical minds of the Catholic tradition — St. John of the Cross and St. Teresa of Avila — learned much about their mystical journey from Islam as it was received into the Spanish Moorish tradition.

Much can be learned from the way Hazrat Pir teaches. Ideally, a student should think: "I will commit myself not to the idea but the process of mastering my own mind and if enough of us do the same 'the world' will simultaneously change because 'the world' is us." A simple way of stating a complicated process, but it is a beginning.

This series of essays, scripts of lectures given by Hazrat Pir discusses his teaching as it relates to the history of Sufism, peace, wisdom, knowledge, healing, meditation, love, prayer, balance, and alchemy. The author, Hazrat Pir Molana Salaheddin Ali Nader Shah Angha, is the forty-second master of Maktab Tarighat Oveyssi Shahmaghsoudi *(School of Islamic Sufism)*, a school that traces its lineage back to the very advent of Islam in the seventh century A.D. While Hazrat Pir's lectures are faithful to the tradition which produced him and which he now guides, they also reflect the mark he has made on that tradition. Raised and trained in the esoteric tradition of Sufism and educated in the West, Hazrat Pir is exceptionally sensitive to the modern world. Accomplished in the disciplines of religion, science, philosophy and poetry, and trained by his father, Molana Hazrat Shah Maghsoud Sadegh Angha (Professor Angha), himself a great master of Sufism and an advanced physicist, Hazrat Pir has, from a very young age developed not only a perceptive and accomplished mind, but also an expansive spirit.

Our desire to transform the world, he teaches, must begin with a transformation of "i" into "I", the true Self. To the Sufi, this necessitates a dialogue between heart and mind. What Westerners call internal learning, or self-knowledge is, to the Sufi, more like a glorified "i" short of a transformation into Self. For example, Hazrat Pir teaches that drug addiction, the scourge of modern society, will elude well-meaning people's attempts to eradicate it, until they understand how to heal the mind of its addiction, and discover the stable "I". To heal the mind of its addiction, one must acknowledge that God, and not the ego is at the center of the "I". Only then is one capable of living a healthy and balanced life.

A serious scrutiny of Hazrat Pir's example would serve the purpose of welcoming a science of mind that may well complement the existing one in the West. Islam is much in the news these days and concerned people want to know more about a culture that is at once alien and familiar — as familiar as the lines from the *Holy Qur'an,* "I am closer to you than your jugular vein." Most Westerners would not have ever read these words unless they were familiar with a poem of the same name by French writer James Sacré. Yet there is a certain basic sanity about those words rooted in a deeper source than that of the creative ego. Heirs of the Greek tradition, the West is only beginning to realize why the heart of Islam seems so close — it has always been there, part of its world, part of its culture, part of its "I" from the beginning.

So it seems fitting that on American soil, a nation founded on the spirit of exploration and discovery, Hazrat Pir has designed and built a memorial in memory of his teacher and father, Professor Angha. In three dimensions, near Novato, California stands a wonderful metaphor for 1400 years of spiritual labor and the integration of the human being's consciousness. There in architecture and here in words on the page, Hazrat Pir encourages the seeker to submit to his or her own metamorphosis and flower like the art of the memorial through the integration of Self, through integrity to the final union with God.

Sufism

He is the Truth, He is the Exalted

Hope is planted seed in fertile ground that bears fruit
In the land of my heart the plant of despair never grows.

The Secret Word

*Y*ou may ask, "What relevance does this have to Sufism?"
The above words may seem poetical, but they constitute
the essence of Sufi teachings. Before explaining this, it may
be of interest to you to know some of the theories presented
by scholars as to the origin of Sufism.

From one perspective we can say that Sufism dates as
far back as the first human being who cognized God. On the
other hand, we can say that Sufism is Islam. I will explain
both perspectives as we move along.

Sufism is the essence of the Prophets' teachings. It is
the Way of the Prophets. It has existed since the beginning of
human history, for its seed lies within every human heart. In
each age, God has sent Prophets to lead people to the knowledge of the "Him" — Zoroaster, Moses, Buddha, Jesus,

9

David, Muhammad — to name a few. Each Prophet has brought humanity a unique instruction to be learned and mastered in order to progress on the inward journey toward "God". The great ninth century Sufi, Bayazid Bastami, described the history of Sufism by stating, "Its seeds were set at the time of Adam, they sprouted under Noah and flowered under Abraham. Grapes formed at the time of Moses, and they ripened at the time of Jesus. In the time of Muhammad, they were made into pure wine."[1]

The following is a summary of the various theories presented by scholars about the origins of Sufism. Some sources relate Sufism's origins as having been influenced by the Hindu Fakirs, relating the ascetic practices of the fakirs to that of the Sufis.[2] Others see it as an outgrowth of Buddhism, because of the similarities found in some of the customs of the Sufis and Buddhist sects, as well as the extensive use of visions in both.[3] They also find similarity in the lives of the Buddha and one of the renowned Sufi Masters, Ibrahim Adham. They were both princes who left everything behind in order to find the Absolute. The Japanese scholar Toshihiko Izutsu endeavored to show similarities between Buddhism and other Far Eastern beliefs and practices, such as the link between Taoism, and Sufism.[4]

Others trace the roots of Sufism to Christianity,[5] seeing similarities between the austerity of the Syrian monks and that of the Sufis. While both Christian monks and

Sufis have sought to distance themselves from superficial attractions of the world, there is an important difference in attitude between the two. Whereas the Christian monks withdrew into monasteries to avoid temptation, the Sufis did not need to abandon the world in such a physical sense; it was their practice to overcome their worldly desires so that their physical environment would have no influence upon them. As my grandfather, Hazrat Mir Ghotbeddin Mohammad Angha has said, "Be among people, but do not partake of their bad habits." And the Holy Prophet Muhammad (peace and blessings upon him) has said, "People are like stones brought to shore. It is when they brush against each other that their sharp edges are smoothed out." Furthermore, the *Holy Qur'an (57:27)* explicitly states that there should be no monasticism in Islam: "But the monasticism which they invented for themselves, We did not prescribe for them."

Quite a few British scholars have said that Sufism was influenced by Neoplatonism. The flaw in this statement will become evident as I explain Sufism. Others argue that Islam began in an area where both ancient Oriental and Christian influences were great, thereby influencing Islam from its onset. These theories first of all show how little these scholars know about the reality of religion, and second, the entire concept of revelation upon which Islam is founded is denied. Social, cultural, ethnic and tribal influences which shape and form religion by the hands of people are mistaken for the genuine message of religion.

Sufism is generally accepted to be the mystical dimension of Islam. Hujwiri,[6] in the 11th century, presented several views of the origin of the term, "Sufi." Some scholars said that Sufism is derived from the word *ahl-suffa* — the People of the Bench — which refers to the platform on which the Holy Prophet Muhammad and the believers used to sit while worshipping God. Others say that they were named Sufis because of their habit of wearing *suf* (wool). The habit of wearing wool next to the skin dates back to the first masters of Islamic Sufism. But while this theory of the derivation of the word does have a foundation in the practices of Sufism, the words of Hazrat Mir Ghotbeddin Mohammad Angha clarify this point: "While every Sufi wears wool, not every person who wears wool — *suf* — is a Sufi." And yet others have concluded that Sufis were named Sufis because of the *safa* — purity — of their hearts and the cleanliness of their actions. Therefore, the practitioners of *safa* are called Sufis, meaning "pure-hearted." What historians have eluded to is not incorrect, but it is incomplete. They have presented the outer form of Sufism, while its inner meaning has been beyond their personal experience.

If we look closely at the last three hypotheses we will note that to be called a Sufi had certain requirements. To be a companion of the Prophet surely requires a different mode of action and behavior. It requires purity of heart, spiritual awareness, and sacredness of goal. In essence, the People of the Bench, or the companions of the Holy Prophet, must have been aware of the significance of the teachings of the Holy Prophet, and must have been intent on being trained by him, because they wanted to know God. Thus, if wearing wool was one of the conditions, they did so. Wearing wool was a mere reminder not to surrender to earthly absorptions. The aim was to reach a state of purity, through which they would be in direct relationship with God, unite with God, be annihilated in God, and subsist in God, and then attest to the Oneness of God — as the Holy Prophet had declared, *la-ilaha-illa'llah*. Reaching this state means that no other but God is in one's heart — *safa*.

This method of purification through submission to God, and annihilation in God was termed *ma'rifa*, meaning acquaintance and cognition. If we want to be exact, the actual word for Sufism is *irfan*, derived from the word *ma'rifa*. Cognition refers to a state whereby nothing remains unknown to us about the subject of inquiry. In this context it refers to the cognition of oneself and the cognition of God. The one who teaches this method of cognition is known as the *arif* — he who has attained the most exalted state of existence through annihilation and permanence in God. The esoteric wisdom of cognition was transmitted from the Holy Prophet to his cousin and son in-law Ali ibn Abu Talib known as Amir al-Mo'menin (peace be upon him). With the assassination of Imam Ali (peace be upon him), the Umayyads came to power, a dynasty whose members were known for their worldliness and impious behavior.

However, the sanctity of the message of Islam and the tradition of the Holy Prophet were kept intact through an unbroken chain of transmission by the great masters of Maktab Tarighat Oveyssi Shahmaghsoudi. While mainstream Islam fell into the hands of the clerics and jurists, these masters passed on the inner message of Islam through their teachings, writings, and students. Islam would not have survived had it not been for the selfless sacrifice of these great spiritual leaders.

The name Oveyssi School is due to a renowned master Oveys Gharani (Uways al-Qarani), whose way of inward cognition was confirmed by the Holy Prophet Muhammad. Therefore, I will start the chronological history of this School with a brief biography of him. Hazrat Oveys Gharani was born in a village called Gharan, close to Najd in Yemen. He was killed in the war of Saffeyn led by Imam Ali, in the year 37/657. Ibn Batoute, the historian, mentioned that his tomb was in Damascus. It is recorded that the Holy Prophet would face Yemen and say: "The breath of the Merciful comes to me from Yemen."[7] The Holy Prophet had his Cloak sent to Hazrat Oveys, an event signifying his holy dignity. Hazrat Oveys' way of cognition was confirmed as the Holy Prophet

Muhammad said: "Follow the way of Oveys.", and "He is the pre-emptor of my genus." Hazrat Oveys' famous aphorism is, "Keep thy heart."

One of the first to be initiated into the Sufi tradition was a Persian from Isfahan called Rouzbeh, son of Khoshnoudan, who was related to King Manuchehr. A Zoroastrian who had converted to Christianity, when he met the Holy Prophet in the city of Medina, he became a Moslem. He became famous as Salman Farsi, and holds a high position in the history of Islam. The Prophet of Islam called him a member of his own family. Salman's passing occurred in 36/656, and his tomb is by the Tigris River in Baghdad, Iraq.

After Hazrat Oveys and Salman Farsi, Hazrat Habib-ibn Salim Ra'i took on the necessary task of leading the people to the right course and gave the disciples instructions in Islam through the inward method of cognition. His successor was Hazrat Soltan Ebrahim Adham, a prince from Balkh who gave up his reign for the path of worship and self-discipline. Trained in the discipline of Sufism by Hazrat Habib-ibn Ra'i, he also served Imam Mohammad Bagher (peace be upon him), the fifth Imam of the Shi'a. The existing Sufi orders of Adhamieh and Choshtieh (Chisti) in India are traced to him. The year of his passing is recorded as 160/776.

The successor of Ibrahim Adham was Hazrat Abu Ali Shaqiq al-Balkhi, who served as companion to Imam Moussa Kazem (peace be upon him), the seventh Imam of the Shi'a.

According to some sources he was martyred for being a Shi'a in 154/770 or 174/790. His successor was Hazrat Sheikh Abu Torab Nakhshabi, who was a nobleman of Khorasan, known for his asceticism. He trained such eminent devotees as Abi Amr al-Istakhri and Abu Abdollah Jalai. He was followed by Hazrat Sheikh Abi Amr al-Istakhri, who passed away about 300/ 912; and then Hazrat Abu Ja'far Hazza, who succeeded him during the era of the Deylamian dynasty in Shiraz. He is one of the eminent masters of the School. He passed away in 341/950, and his tomb is located in Shiraz, Iran.

Hazrat Sheikh Kabir Abu Abdollah Mohammad-ibn Khafif Shirazi was the next in the line of succession. This great master of the School, who lived during the 4th/11th century, developed a special method of training, now known as Khafifieh Oveyssieh. He was followed by Hazrat Sheikh Hossein Akkar, whose full name was Hossein ibn Mohammad al-Houri al-Firouzabadi. He guided many on the path of self-knowledge, including an eminent devotee named Sheikh Morshed Abu-Isshaq Shahriar Kazerouni, who became his successor. He attained the highest state of cognition in Sufism, passed away in 391/1000, and is entombed in Shiraz.

Sheikh Morshed Abu-Isshaq Shahriar Kazerouni was born in Navard, a village of Kazeroun, in 356/966. He was a contemporary of al-Ghader Bellah, an Abassid Caliph. His training began at the age of 15, and he attained the highest state of cognition and was given the Holy Cloak at the age of twenty. Because of his well-known efforts to propagate Islamic Sufism, he was also called Sheikh the Judge. He passed away in 426/1034 in Kazeroun, and was buried in Ganjabad.

His successor was Hazrat Khatib Abolfath Abdolkarim, known as a scientist, who passed away in 442/1050. He was followed by Hazrat Ali- ibn Hassan Basri, who spent most of his life in Egypt. His successor was Hazrat Serajeddin Abolfath Mahmoud-ibn Mahmoudi Sabouni Beyzavi. Born in Baghdad in 500/1106, he traveled to Damascus and then to Egypt, where he was received by King Najmeddin Ayub, father of Salaheddin. He remained in Egypt until the end of his life. He trained his successor Hazrat Sheikh Abu Abdollah Rouzbehan Baghli Shirazi, who is considered one of the most illustrious masters of Sufism. Of the many books he wrote, *Fidele D'Amour* is best known in the West. He passed away in 606/1209, and his tomb is located in Shiraz, Iran, in a district called Gate of the Sheikh.

He was succeeded by Hazrat Sheikh Najmeddin Tamat-al Kobra Khivaghi, the greatest sage and Sufi of his time. He trained seventeen noble disciples. Among them were Sheikh Farideddin Attar, Seyfeddin Bakharzi, and Ali Lala Ghaznavi — who succeeded him. Molana Jalaleddin Balkhi Rumi was a student of one of Hazrat Kobra's disciples. He was martyred by Mongols in 618/1221, when he was seventy eight years old.

Hazrat Ali Lala Ghaznavi was succeeded by Hazrat Sheikh Ahmad Zaker Jowzeghani who founded the *zikr* (chants of remembrance) of *la-ilaha-illa'llah* (there is no other but God). He passed away in 669/1270 in the era of Ebgha Khan, son of Holaku Khan, and his tomb is in Kurian-Esfarayen, Iran.

He was succeeded by his son, Hazrat Noureddin Abdolrahman Esfarayeni, whom he trained from an early age to reach the highest level of cognition in Sufism. He wrote prolificly and endeavored greatly to introduce Sufism to the people of his time. He passed away in 717/1317 in Baghdad. He had trained Hazrat Sheikh Alaoddowleh Semnani to be his successor. Hazrat Semnani, who was born to a wealthy and noble family in Semnan, Iran, studied the sciences of his time, and entered the royal court at an early age. While serving in the war of Arghon-Khan, he felt a revolution in himself and began his search for cognition through worship and self-discipline. After meeting his master, Hazrat Noureddin Esfarayeni, he attained the highest state of cognition and then propagated the teachings and wrote numerous works. He passed away in 736/1335 in Borj-Ahrar Sufi Abad, Iran.

He trained Hazrat Mahmoud Mazdeghani, who was considered the greatest Sufi of the 8th/15th century, to be his successor. Hazrat Amir Seyyed Ali Hamedani, known as the second Ali, was renowned for his knowledge of the sciences and Sufism. He wrote many works and succeeded his master, Hazrat Mazdeghani.

Hazrat Sheikh Ahmad Khatlani attained the highest state of cognition through his master, Hazrat Seyyed Ali Hamedani. At the age of ninety six, by the order of Mirza Shahrokh, he was martyred in Balkh for being a Shi'a.

Hazrat Seyyed Mohammad Abdollah Ghatifi al-Hasavi Nourbakhsh was an eminent personality and the Sufi of his time. Born in Gha'en in the district of Ghohestan, he was granted the title of Nourbakhsh (one who bestows light) by his master, Hazrat Khatlani. His books and treatises are detailed in *Research, Biography, and Works of Mohammad Nourbakhsh*. He passed away in 869/1464, and his tomb is located in Souleghan, Iran. He trained Hazrat Shah Ghassem Feyzbakhsh to be his successor. Hazrat Feyzbakhsh, who was praised and highly respected by Shah Ismail Safavi, king of Iran, passed away in 927/1520. The next four masters, in succession, were Hazrat Hossein Abarghoui Janbakhsh, Hazrat Darvish Malek Ali Joveyni, Hazrat Darvish Ali Sodeyri, and Hazrat Darvish Kamaleddin Sodeyri, who was succeeded by Hazrat Darvish Mohammad Mozaheb Karandehi (known as Pir Palandouz). This great master was born in the 10th/17th century, and passed away in 1037/1627. His tomb is located in Mashad, Iran.

The next masters, again in succession, were Hazrat Mir Mohammad Mo'men Sodeyri Sabzevari, Hazrat Mir

Mohammad Taghi Shahi Mashhadi, Hazrat Mir Mozafar Ali, Hazrat Mir Mohammad Ali, Hazrat Seyyed Shamseddin Mohammad, and Hazrat Seyyed Abdolvahab Naini, who was a renowned master from Yazd, Iran. He passed away at the age of ninety six, in the year 1212/1797, and his tomb is located in Nain, Iran.

Hazrat Haj Mohammad Hassan Kouzekanani was his successor. Born in Kouzekanan, Tabriz, in 1156/1743, he passed away in Nain in 1250/1834. In *Nassekh al-Tavarikh* is recorded the famous story of how he met with Mohammad Shah Ghajar when Mohammad was a young prince. He gave Mohammad a sword, saying that he would become king of Iran. Several years later when Mohammad became king, he realized it was only because Hazrat Kouzekanani had given him the sword. He was followed by Hazrat Agha Abdolghader Jahromi.

After Sheikh Jahromi, an important event took place in the history of the School. Hazrat Jalaleddin Ali Mir Abolfazl Angha, in addition to receiving the leadership in the Oveyssi order from Hazrat Jahromi, was given authority of succession by both Hazrat Agha Mohammad Jassebi to the Maroufi, Nematollahi order, and by Hazrat Seyyed Hossein Dezfuli to the Zahabieh order, becoming the Pole of his time. Born in Ghazvin in 1266/1849, he came to Tehran in 1284/1867 and attained the absolute state of cognition through hard work, obedience, and discipline. He began explaining Sufism in scientific terms. He passed away in Tehran in 1339/1915.

Hazrat Mir Ghotbeddin Mohammad Angha succeeded his father and attained a supreme position in science and Sufism. It is written of Hazrat Mir Ghotbeddin that, "If it were not for our Lord Mohammad, son of Mir Abolfazl Angha, the reality of Sufism would never have appeared in our era." Born in Tehran on May 10, 1887, he passed away on September 22, 1962, and is buried next to his father.

My father, Hazrat Shah Maghsoud Sadegh Angha, succeeded his father as the forty first great master of the School. Because of his immense knowledge in so many fields and because he made Sufism accessible to the contemporary person through his voluminous writings in the sciences, philosophy, poetry, alchemy, etc., the School is now known as Maktab Tarighat Oveyssi Shahmaghsoudi. His teaching marked the advent of a new era in the history of Sufism. The truth of Islam was to be made world known. The knowledge embedded in the teachings of the *Holy Qur'an*, and the traditions of the Holy Prophet were to be announced to humanity. On September 4, 1970 my father officially appointed me as his successor, and gave me the responsibility to propagate this message to the human community.

It may seem to you that what I have said so far is history. However, if you look closely, you will discover that I have presented the fundamental points upon which Sufism rests. You will note that confirmation and appointment of each master by his predecessor is an absolute necessity. Let us take the example of Hazrat Oveys. Although he never met the Holy Prophet on the physical plane, he was nonetheless confirmed by the Holy Prophet. Hazrat Salman Farsi was directly trained and confirmed by the Holy Prophet. Each of these great masters represents a different aspect of the teachings of this School. First, the necessity of the presence of the master, and second, the inward attainment of cognition. The other important point which must not be forgotten is that this chain of transmission has never been broken from the time of the Holy Prophet to the present time, which means the light and knowledge of Islam has never been left unguarded. Just as the sun never ceases to shine, this knowledge too has been passed from master to master, so those who seek to attain their divine state will be guided toward such a goal.

Knowledge of the truth of the human being and existence has a course which goes beyond the basic preliminary messages and discoveries, and ends with absolute cognition. This innate drive and curiosity has determined the human being's destiny and fate and has completed the pages of self-knowledge with the humming love-call of its seekers throughout the centuries. In each age, according to the will of Existence, a new branch appears on the tree of Life — the pre-emptor — to guide and save the sons of man.

Existence created the beautiful in manifestations, and beauty has been veiled in meaning. As it is stated in the *Holy Qur'an, 2:257*: "God is the protector of those who have faith: from the depths of darkness He will lead them forth unto light."

Now, I would like to speak on the experiential aspect of this transmitted knowledge of Sufism and its relevance for each person and for human societies — a reality for each one of you. I have defined Sufism as the reality of religion, the true human right of each person in his own time and the way to the realization of human perfection. If we separate human prejudices and cultural factors from the essence of the message of the Prophets we will see that the message of each is intended to direct human beings to experience a higher state of their being. However, the only thing that remains from the teachings of the Prophets is a set of empty rituals, superstition and dogma that no intelligent human being is willing to accept. The noble and dignified rank of religion has been lost in the cobweb of the ignorance of those who claim to represent the Holy Prophets. The decadence and outdated systems of existing spiritual institutions have fostered alienation and disinterest in people. Religion has become a means of mobilizing masses of ignorant and underprivileged people by promising them heaven or threatening them with hell. Religion in societies is no more than social gatherings or political platforms, instead of being institutions where people are introduced to their true human dignity and are taught to be the true peacemakers of societies.

Interfaith gatherings have become quite popular. Groups gather to discuss how they must understand each other in order to prevent religious conflicts and wars. But, they do not ask themselves, why is it that in a family, or society or country where one religion prevails, there are so many conflicts, hatreds, and killings? They fail to realize that the most fundamental purpose of religion is to transform human beings from their base level to their divine level of existence. If religion truly existed in the lives of people, then greed, struggle for power and fame, envy, jealousy, etc., which are the sources for the many conflicts in the world, would not exist.

How many times have we seen the boundaries of nations drawn and redrawn? How many wars have erupted in societies and devastated and destroyed the lives of people? How many civilizations have become mere ruins because of invasions?

John Foster Dulles, among others, has said that there has been a war every three years out of four in the history of man. The number of organizations promoting peace has increased dramatically, yet the number of tribal, regional, religious conflicts has not decreased. It is estimated that the number of violent deaths in the 20th century is close to 100 million.

What type of societies are we speaking about when we read in the headlines: "Youth Kill Youth," "Getting Ready to Die Young: Surrounded by Violence, Some D.C. Youths Plan Their Own Funerals," "Youth Gets Two Life Terms in Baby Killing," "Specialists See a Youthful Version of Battered Spouse Syndrome." In the U.S.A., for example, the polls show that the first concern of the American people is crime! The spirit of despair is becoming pervasive in societies. Youth have lost their hope and respect for institutions, leaders, parents, and teachers, because they see the confusion, the corruption, the inconsistencies that engulf their societies. Why is humanity so helpless to achieve a conclusive peace and harmonious and tranquil societies? What will it take for humans to realize that they must look at peace from a different perspective?

The basic unit of any society is the human being. If this unit is not known, how then can effective laws, programs, structures, educational, economic systems be devised to meet its needs? As I mentioned earlier, the correct word for Sufism is *irfan*, derived from the word *ma'rifa*, which means to know, to cognize. When can we say we know something? When nothing about the subject of study remains unknown to us.

Is it not amazing that with such extensive research being conducted in the biological, behavioral, social, psychological sciences, no conclusive results in knowing this complex organism have yet been attained? The intricate mechanism and functions of this organism, which has an average volume of somewhat more than a cubic yard and weighs an average of 170 pounds, are so complex that one expert is unable to diagnose all its aspects individually. Separate specialized branches and sub-specialties had to be developed to give a more complete assessment of each aspect.

Over 1,400 years ago the Prophet of Islam said, "Whoever cognizes the true self has cognized God." The true self is not the changing cellular system, the social conditionings, nor the mental and emotional states that are constantly in a state of flux and change. The true self is the stable reality, the true personality of each human being. In Islam it is equated with the Divine. This is why Islam proclaims the Oneness of Existence — *la-ilaha-illa'llah* — there is no other but God." This is the true human dignity granted to humans, that there is no separation between you and God. As it is stated in the *Holy Qur'an (50:16)*, "I am closer to you than your jugular vein."

Religion is a discipline, a precise system of training, whereby each person is individually trained to discover a dimension within his or her own being where the divine attributes are manifested. It is the realization of attributes such as compassion, knowledge, selflessness, love, devotion, honor, trust, etc., attributes normally associated with saints of the past. This is the dimension of their being that the Prophets discovered through their cognition of God that gave rise to their uniqueness, strength, and knowledge.

When people are trained to discover this inner dimension of their being, then willingly they will leave behind their savage attributes which give rise to greed, injustice, hatred and violence. What is the result of such a discovery? If each person is trained to stand on his or her own strength, will they be needy? Will they not see their own uniqueness and the strength that this uniqueness brings? If each person is trained to develop his or her own talents and abilities, will there be any room for insecurity, jealousy, or envy? Will they be lacking anything? Will they need to compete with anyone?

In 1973, sixteen scientific questions were addressed to my father by the International Multidisciplinary Research Association.[8] The questions posed by these scientists centered around major problems of modern science which are of critical importance to the improvement of the mental and physical well-being of humanity, to ecological harmony, and even to the actual continuation of human life on this planet. Several questions concerned competition: "Why do organisms compete with one another instead of cooperating (or loving, as in the case of humans)?" They asked why trees competed and killed one another for a place in the sun, why wouldn't they form one great organism, and why do individual parts of organisms accept the influence of other parts, but collectively continue to struggle? The question is quite lengthy and ultimately leads to inter-cellular communication and healing, a topic which would require a lengthy discussion and cannot be discussed at this time.

I think my father's response to these scientists will clarify many points for you. He stated that if we put the question differently, we might see that all organisms and parts of organisms, are cooperating in life. A particle loses nothing when it is eaten by another. The billions of plants which we conceive of as living separately, is each an agent of life that influences and is influenced and changed by interactions with all other life forms. Each particle continues until unfavorable conditions occur, at which point it is dissolved (we call this death) and then transformed into another form, thus continuing its life anew. Life continues, regardless of the form it may take.

"Perhaps it would be better to say that cellular life lacks competition." In the infinite unity of existence, there are no conflicts and no antagonisms. Humanity, in attempting to explain reality, has sometimes thought that the transient world remains preserved somehow, in some non-material, spiritual form. But the units of measurement accepted by science conceal the spiritual, non-material realm, making it impossible for us to perceive or even conceptualize such a world. For example, water presents contrasting forms depending on its state. We are aware of fluid, ice, or steam, but the true structure of water is concealed. The same is true of all other matter. "Although all matter has different manifestations, their genuine reality is never lost, and nothing is either increased or decreased."

What cell or molecule can feed or struggle beyond its capability? Not a single one; otherwise it would upset the equilibrium of its life. We see ourselves and all matter as being individual, separated and isolated from each other, for our senses prevent us from knowing the essence of our being and the true unity of all existence. In a young tree, we see separate branches and leaves, yet it is nourished through its life span by a root provided by existence, through the unity of being which makes a tree a tree. In appearance we behold the separateness of nature, but infinite existence is the only nurturer, just as it is with the branches and leaves. Everything is interdependent and sustained by the unifying force of existence.

"The world of creation is a painted surface. If everything in the painting were only one color and monotonous, it would not cheer anyone. It is the variety of contrasting colors which cause human beings, animals, plants, and inanimate objects to be worthy of note."

The business community is finally shifting its focus from competition to cooperation. It has now seen that when cooperation exists, productivity and job satisfaction are increased. As a result there is less job turnover, less absenteeism, less job-related stress and stress-induced illnesses. Since cooperation translates into more profit for the company, the business community therefore promotes it.

In a society where children are taught that they must compete in order to get ahead, how can they not be expected to step over others in order to become successful? Are not social structures founded upon race, color, religion, ethnicity, etc.? Aren't these elements used to foster hatred and separation? Isn't it time to see that what appears as diversity is a reflection of an underlying unity, and diversity can be a source for creativity and not conflict? If people are able to see that race, gender, ethnicity have no bearing on human dignity, will so much hatred and animosity exist? After all, does the soul have a gender, race, color or creed?

Hopelessness, insecurities, and strife exist in societies because people have not found the stable source of their existence. During the historical span of time which appears to be so long, the universe has continued with tranquility and peace throughout its orbital revolutions without ever faltering. What law prevails in this nearly infinite journey which governs all entities and their precise interrelationships, and prevents any disorder in their development and evolutionary motion as presented in the manifestation of nature?

Recognition and discovery of this specific principle, the source which causes a relative permanence for such matter and celestial bodies that may appear without "intelligence", may be invaluable in reaching a deeper and more conclusive understanding of peace. Because in Sufism, recognition of the true sense of religion, the ultimate goal of the Holy Prophets and Saints, has been the attainment of an ideal which is synonymous with eternity and final peace. It is stated in the *Holy Qur'an (40:64)*:

> He — God who placed the earth as your foundation and the sky as the axis of your organizer constructed your figure to perfection, and gave you blessed sustenance; This is Allah, your Protector, who is Great — the Protector of mankind.

If we observe the structures of the smallest particle to the largest celestial bodies, we will see that the existence of each entity is founded upon a structure, and yet these structures are hidden to the naked eye. Cognition of God within the heavenly realm of each individual is like a seed that a gardener plants in fertile ground and looks after, day in and day out, until that seed undergoes its complete cycles of growth and bears its fruit.

If you look at the growth process of a seed, you will see that the necessary structure for its evolutionary process to move from seed to fruit was foreseen in the seed itself. The place where the seed grows, and the conditions under which it grows, determine how many of the existing structures are activated into realization. The healthy growth of the root determines the future of the stem, branches, leaves, flower and fruit. Each stage of growth is dependent upon the completion and health of the preceding stage. To manifest its ultimate stage of completion, each stage of growth must be in a state of health, and in harmony with the prevailing environmental conditions.

The human being has a highly developed and intricate structure. Overall, the human being relates and interacts through the following four different levels that comprise his axis of search, thought and being:

First, the mysterious inner level, which is the central point of stability of the human being's character and identity;

Second, the developmental level, which is the locus for the development and interrelationship of the magnetic bodies and for mental, sensory, and psychic powers;

Third, the dependent, indigent and impressed cellular level, which in fact is the mechanical level of the human being;

Fourth, nature, which is the locus for material manifestation and exchange — the laboratory for the examination and experience of man's aptitudes, and the place to satisfy his needs. Each level has different requirements for its existence, and yet is dependent on the previous level for its health and balance. While the physical level needs nature for its sustenance, it is dependent on the health and stability of the electromagnetic system, which in turn is sustained through its connection with the source of life in the heart. My father, Hazrat Shah Maghsoud Sadegh Angha has explained this in detail in his book, *The Hidden Angles of Life*.

If you look closely, you will see that the fragrance of the flower has no resemblance to its roots in the soil, and yet the roots were necessary for the growth of the flower and the presence of the fragrance. The entire growth process was intended for that fragrance to emerge. The fragrance would not have evolved, had the flower not completed its full cycle of growth under stable conditions. Whereas the flower is grounded to the roots through the stem, the fragrance is unbounded and free. For reflective people, nature can be an eloquent teacher showing the laws of Existence.

The prescribed rites of religion are a means for humans to re-establish their connection with their inner level, from which they are estranged. It is stability in this level that frees the soul from being under the domination of the earthly appetites of the human being. The instructions given by the Holy Prophets provide the necessary structure to free the soul from enslavement, so humans may attain their true rank as created in the image of God. The soul is the divine essence present within each human being. Where reliance resides in God, can despair ever be present? What is the fruit of reliance in God, but hope, prosperity, tranquility and peace?

My father has said in his book *Nirvan*, "On the seventh day, man was housed in the Empyrean. A sound of hope echoed in the infinite existence: 'Nonentity is not, and unique Existence is.' Nirvan, who had left the world of appearances, thrust away the dust, lost his identity in the infinite, and regained peace."[9]

How do we measure whether or not what we have done has been effective? By the results we obtain. What is the measurement for knowing we have "religion"? The result of having religion should show in the presence of peace, stability and hope in our lives. Despair and hope cannot reside side by side; nor, can hatred and love; nor, can greed and compassion. Tell me, if you have God, what else do you need? Doesn't 100 include 1 through 99?

My father, in his book *Dawn*, has said, "The wise are those who acquire benefits and repel losses."[10] It is up to each person to decide what he or she wishes to nurture and grow. Existence is infinite, and infinite possibilities are available at each instant for each person. What course do you want to choose on this infinite journey of no return?

May God plant the seed of prosperity, hope and peace in the land of your heart.

Endnotes

1. Quoted in the preface to al-Muqaddisi, Sheikh Izzidin. (1980). *Revelation of the Secrets of the Birds and Flowers*. London: Octagon Press.

2. See Schimmel, Annemarie. (1975). *Mystical Dimensions of Islam*. Chapel Hill: University of North Carolina Press.

3. See Nicholson, Reynold A. (1989). *The Mystics of Islam*. London: Arkana.

4. See Izutsu, Toshihiko, (1994). *Creation and the Timeless Order of Things*. Ashland, OR: White Cloud Press.

5. See, for example, Smith, Margaret. (1978). *The Way of the Mystics*. NY: Oxford University Press.

6. Hujwiri, Ali B. Uthman al-Jullabi. (1978). *Kashf al-Mahjub of al-Hujwiri*. London: E.J.W. Gibb Memorial.

7. *Mystical Dimensions of Islam*, p. 28.

8. The responses to these questions were published in *The Hidden Angles of Life*, by Molana al-Moazam Hazrat Shah Maghsoud Sadegh Angha. (1975). Pomona, CA: Multidisciplinary Publications.

9. Angha, Molana al-Moazam Hazrat Shah Maghsoud Sadegh. (1986). *The Mystery of Humanity: Survival and Tranquility*. Lanham: University Press of America. p. 36.

10. Angha, Molana al-Moazam Hazrat Shah Maghsoud Sadegh. (1989). *Dawn*. Lanham: University Press of America. p. 31.

Genealogy of Maktab Tarighat Oveyssi Shahmaghsoudi
(School of Islamic Sufism)®

Prophet Mohammad
Imam Ali
Hazrat Oveys Gharani*
Hazrat Salman Farsi
Hazrat Habib-ibn Salim Ra'i
Hazrat Soltan Ebrahim Adham
Hazrat Abu Ali Shaqiq al-Balkhi
Hazrat Sheikh Abu Torab Nakhshabi
Hazrat Sheikh Abi Amr al-Istakhri
Hazrat Abu Ja'far Hazza
Hazrat Sheikh Kabir Abu Abdollah Mohammad-ibn Khafif Shirazi
Hazrat Sheikh Hossein Akkar
Hazrat Sheikh Morshed Abu-Isshaq Shahriar Kazerouni
Hazrat Khatib Abolfath Abdolkarim
Hazrat Ali-ibn Hassan Basri
Hazrat Serajeddin Abolfath Mahmoud-ibn Mahmoudi Sabouni Beyzavi
Hazrat Sheikh Abu Abdollah Rouzbehan Baghli Shirazi
Hazrat Sheikh Najmeddin Tamat-al Kobra Khivaghi
Hazrat Sheikh Ali Lala Ghaznavi
Hazrat Sheikh Ahmad Zaker Jowzeghani
Hazrat Noureddin Abdolrahman Esfarayeni
Hazrat Sheikh Alaoddowleh Semnani
Hazrat Mahmoud Mazdaghani
Hazrat Amir Seyyed Ali Hamedani
Hazrat Sheikh Ahmad Khatlani
Hazrat Seyyed Mohammad Abdollah Ghatifi al-Hasavi Nourbakhsh
Hazrat Shah Ghassem Feyzbakhsh
Hazrat Hossein Abarghoui Janbakhsh
Hazrat Darvish Malek Ali Joveyni
Hazrat Darvish Ali Sodeyri
Hazrat Darvish Kamaleddin Sodeyri
Hazrat Darvish Mohammad Mozaheb Karandehi (Pir Palandouz)
Hazrat Mir Mohammad Mo'men Sodeyri Sabzevari
Hazrat Mir Mohammad Taghi Shahi Mashhadi
Hazrat Mir Mozaffar Ali
Hazrat Mir Mohammad Ali
Hazrat Seyyed Shamseddin Mohammad
Hazrat Seyyed Abdolvahab Naini
Hazrat Haj Mohammad Hassan Kouzekanani
Hazrat Agha Abdolghader Jahromi
Hazrat Jalaleddin Ali Mir Abolfazl Angha
Hazrat Mir Ghotbeddin Mohammad Angha
Hazrat Molana Shah Maghsoud Sadegh Angha
Hazrat Salaheddin Ali Nader Shah Angha

The conventional Arabic transliteration is Uways al-Qarani